Kolam - Series 1 : 6x6 parallel dots

Kolam - Series 1 : 6 x 6 parallel dots

Kolam

Joining the dots.
Step by Step in a Easy & Jolly method.
Kids colouring book.

6 by 6 Parallel dots.
Simple every day Kolam.

About the book.

Kolam - Series 1 : 6 x 6 parallel dots

    Kolam or rangoli is an art. In India most of the houses have a Kolam in front of their houses. Before sunrise and sunset women will clean the entrance and draw some kolam. This said to improve the health of a person mentally and physically. Usually this is done with raw rice powder, which will be taken by the ants as food. Even we can use colour powder to improve the presentation. This is a vast area. In this book you can see only "6 by 6 parallel dots for beginners."

    One can find a step by step picture of how to join the dots. This is one of the traditions followed by our ancestors, which has more scientific reason behind it. You will find it more interesting.

OK lets Begin . . .

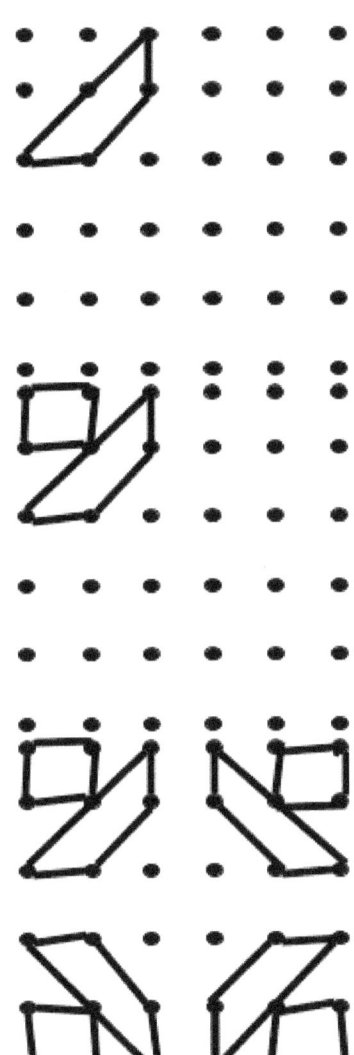

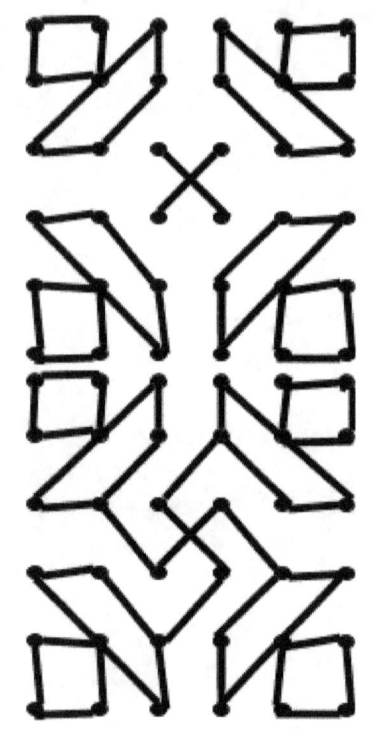

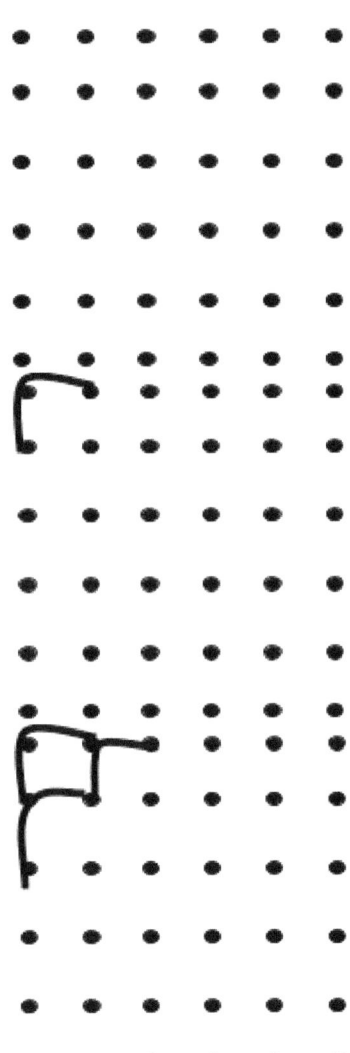

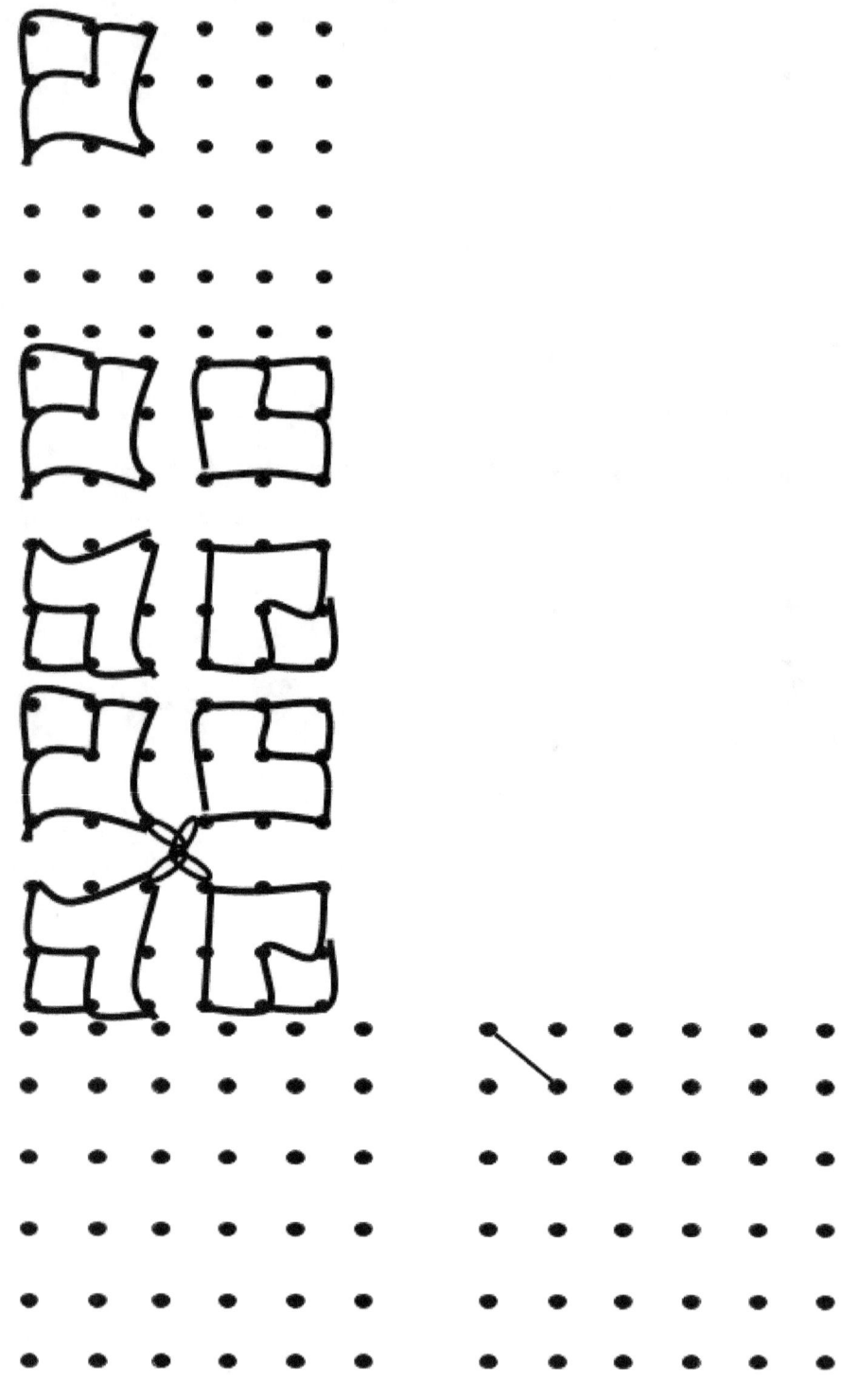

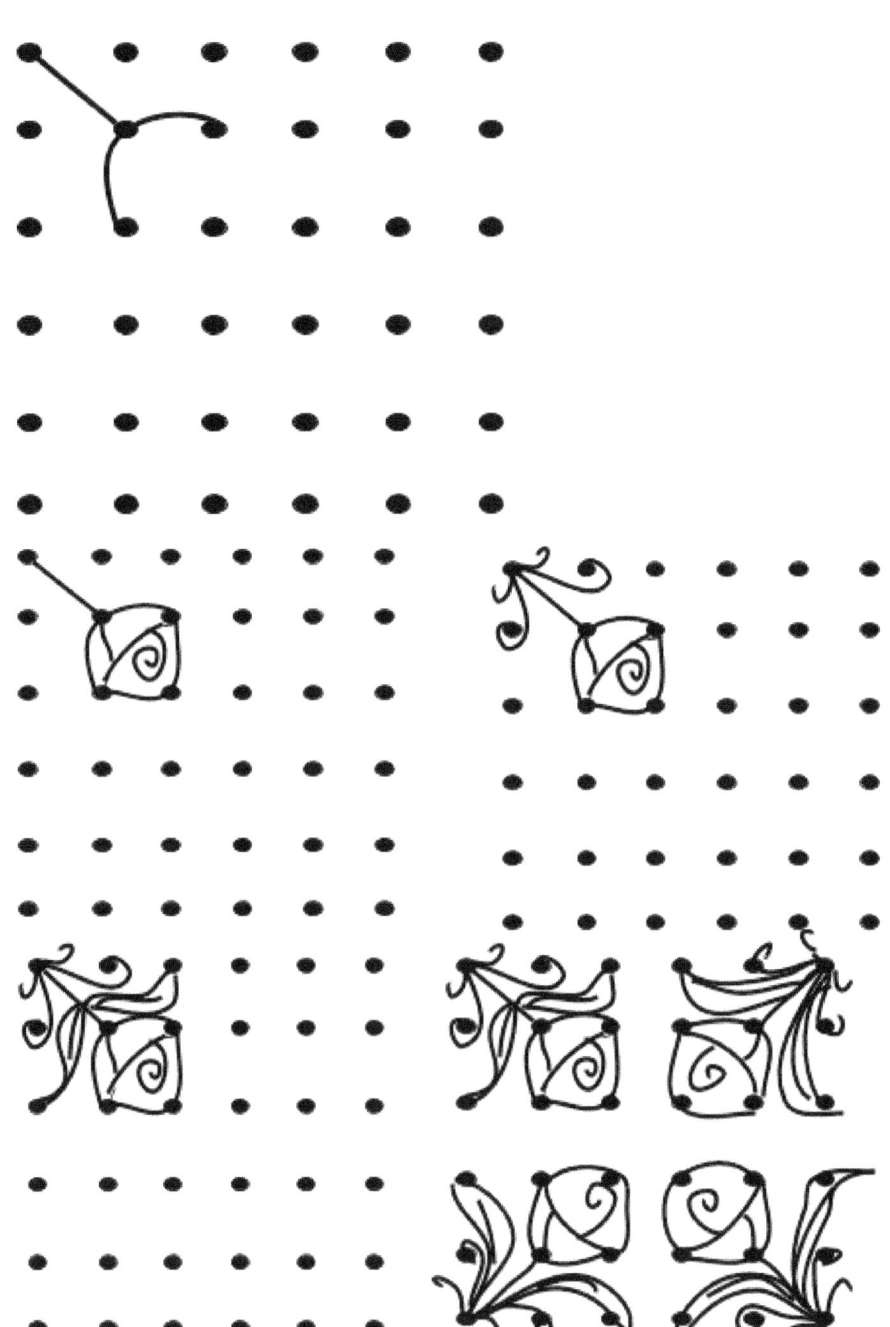

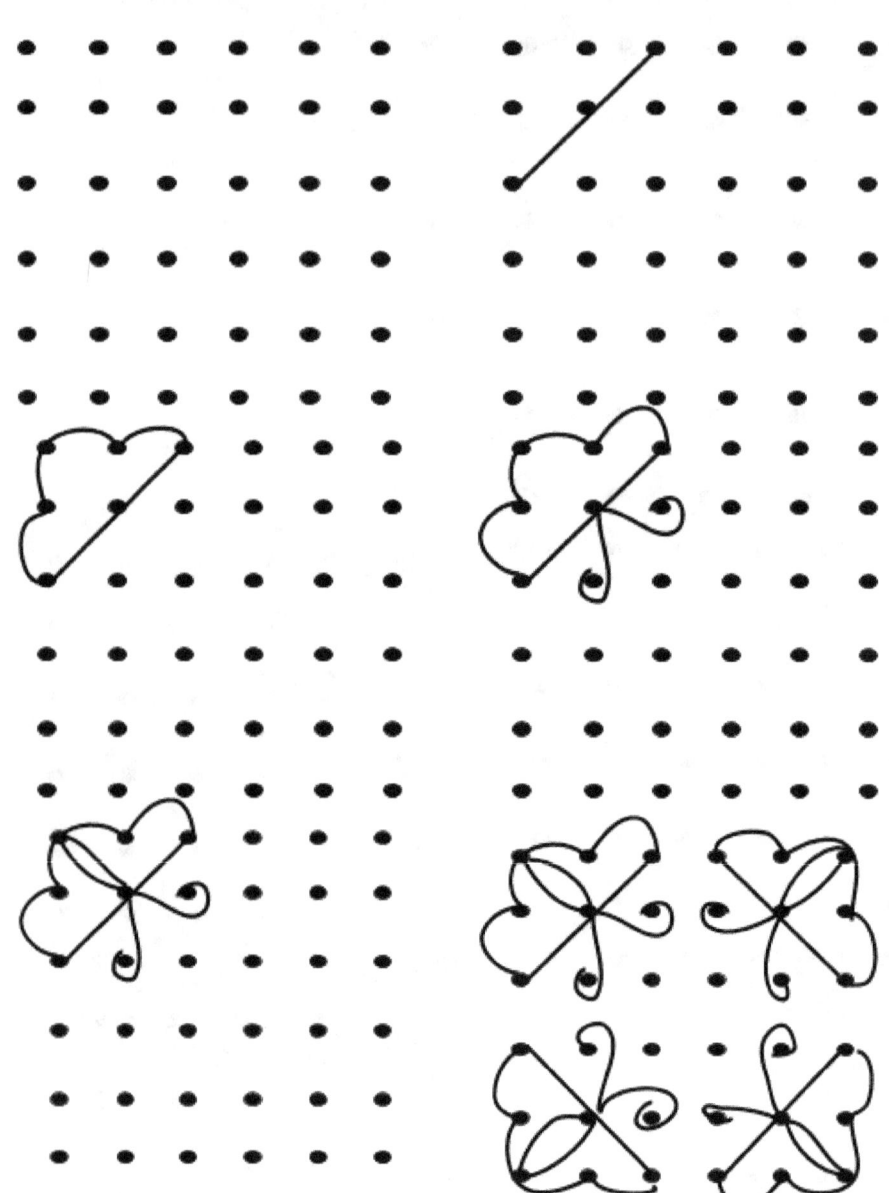

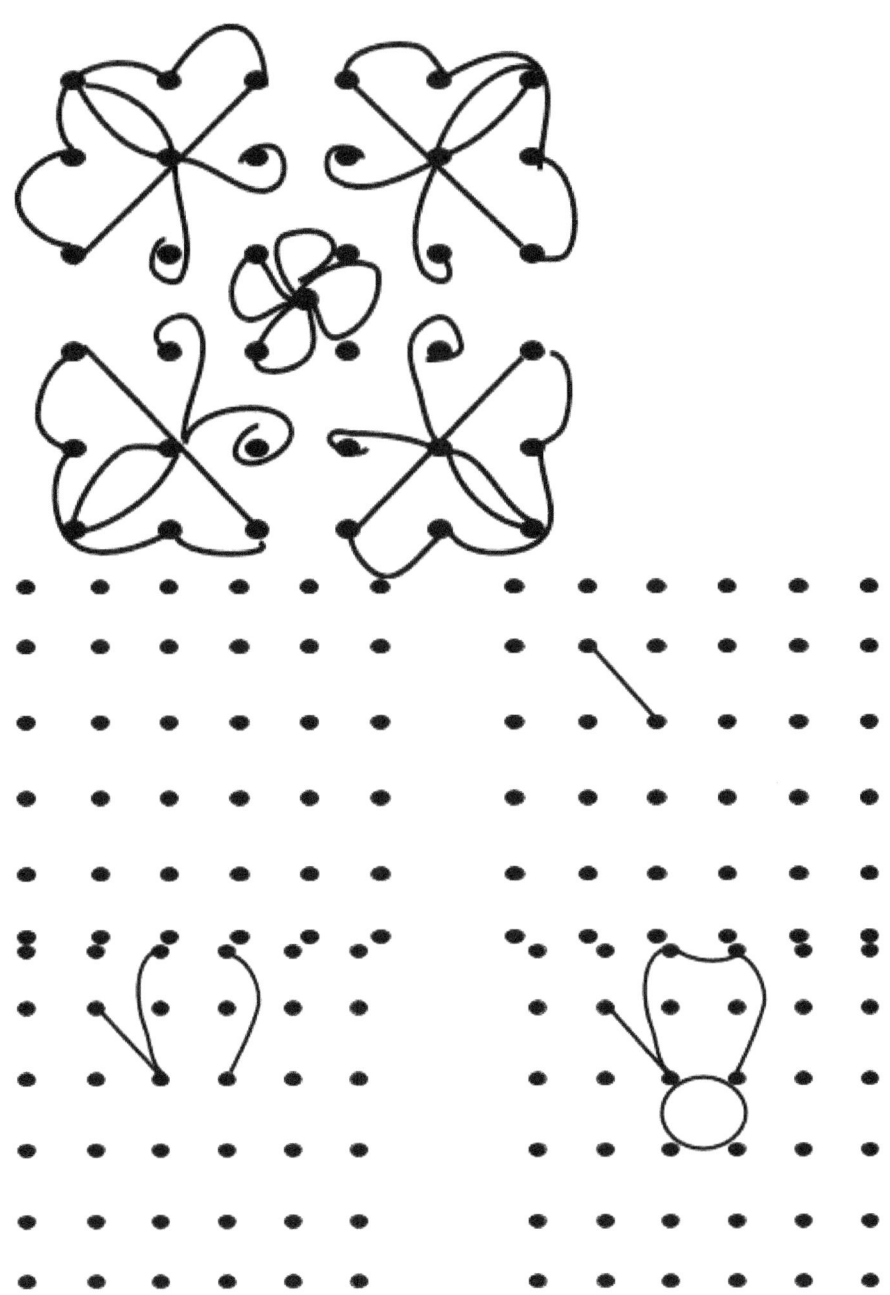

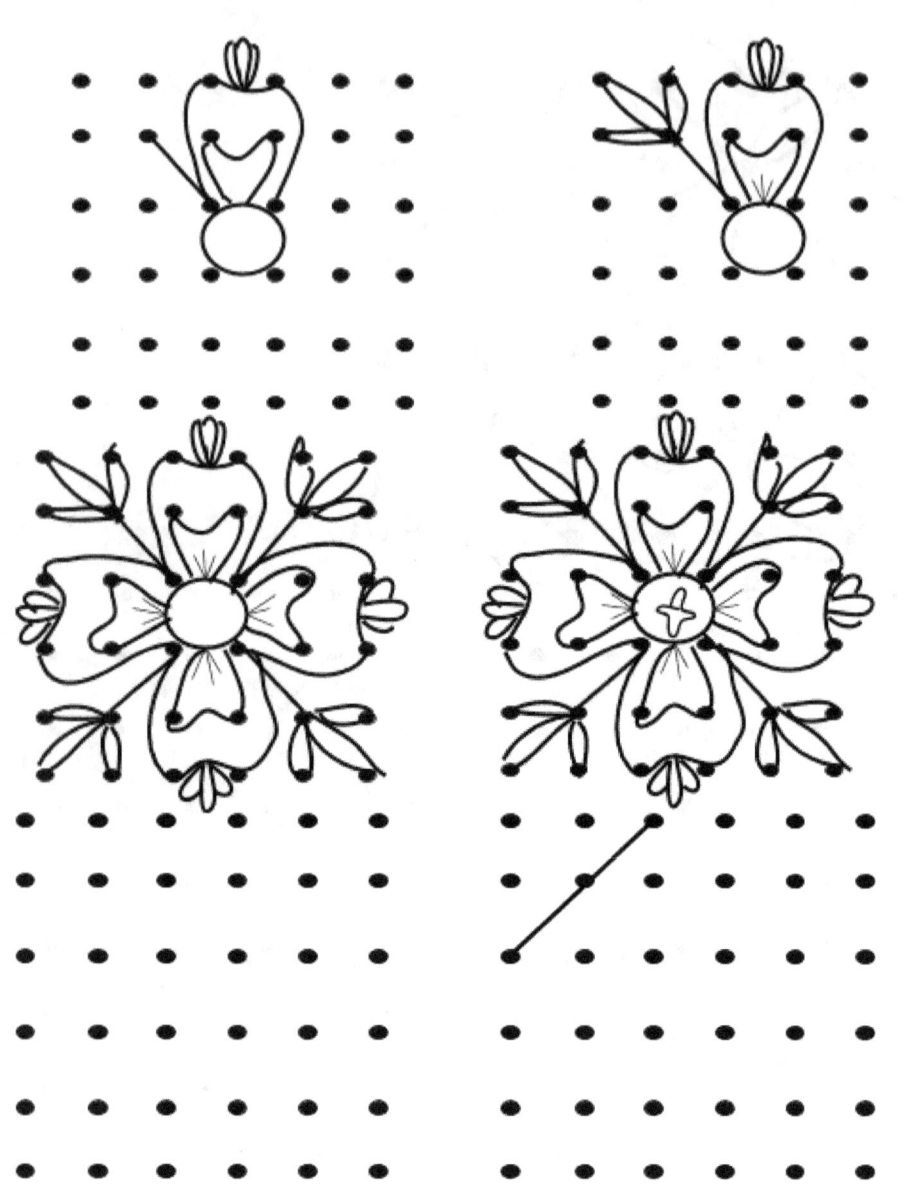

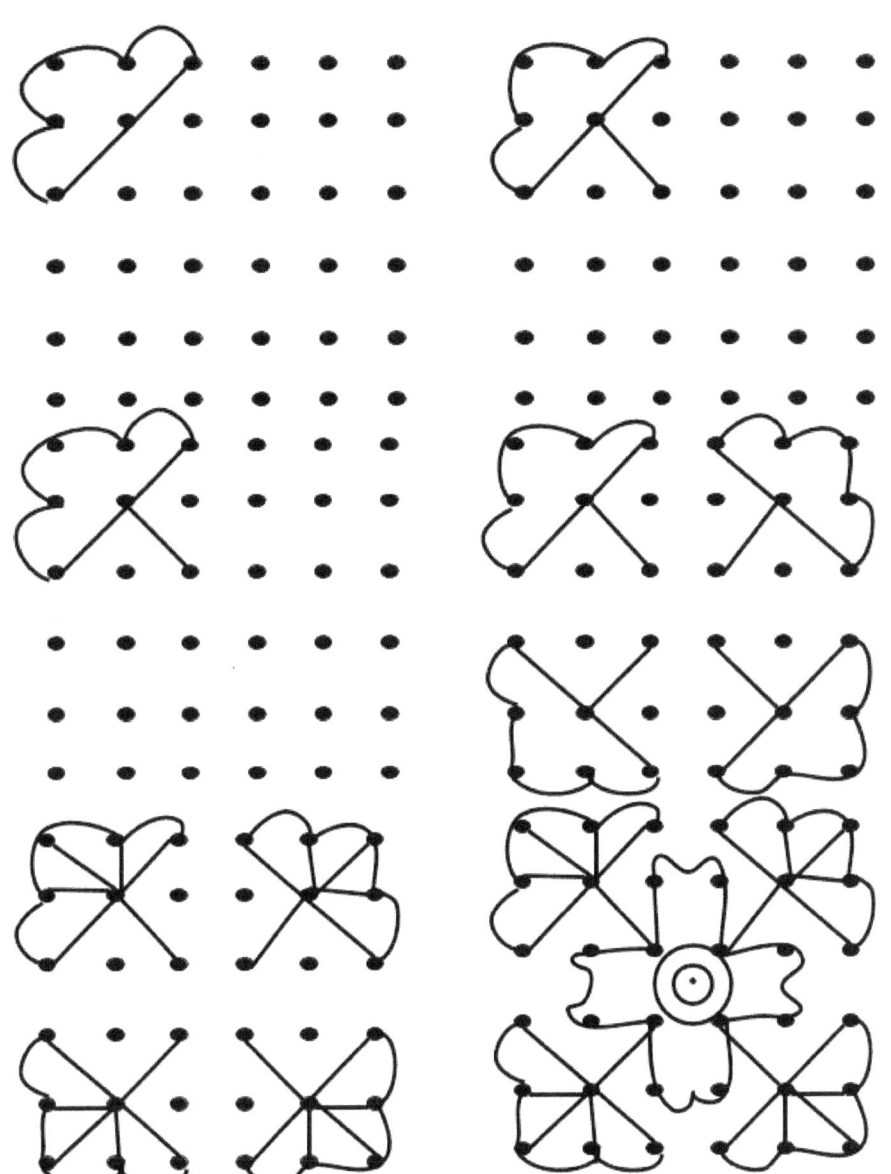

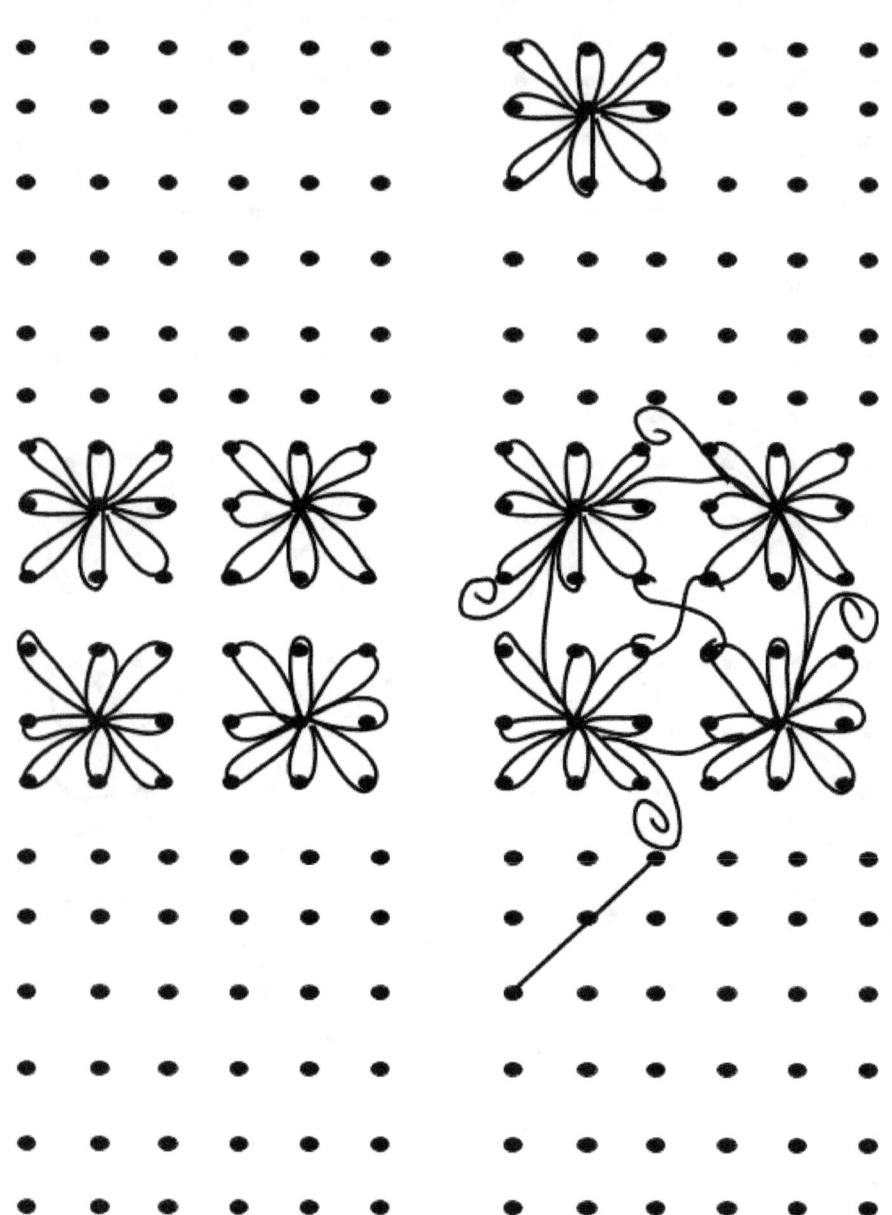

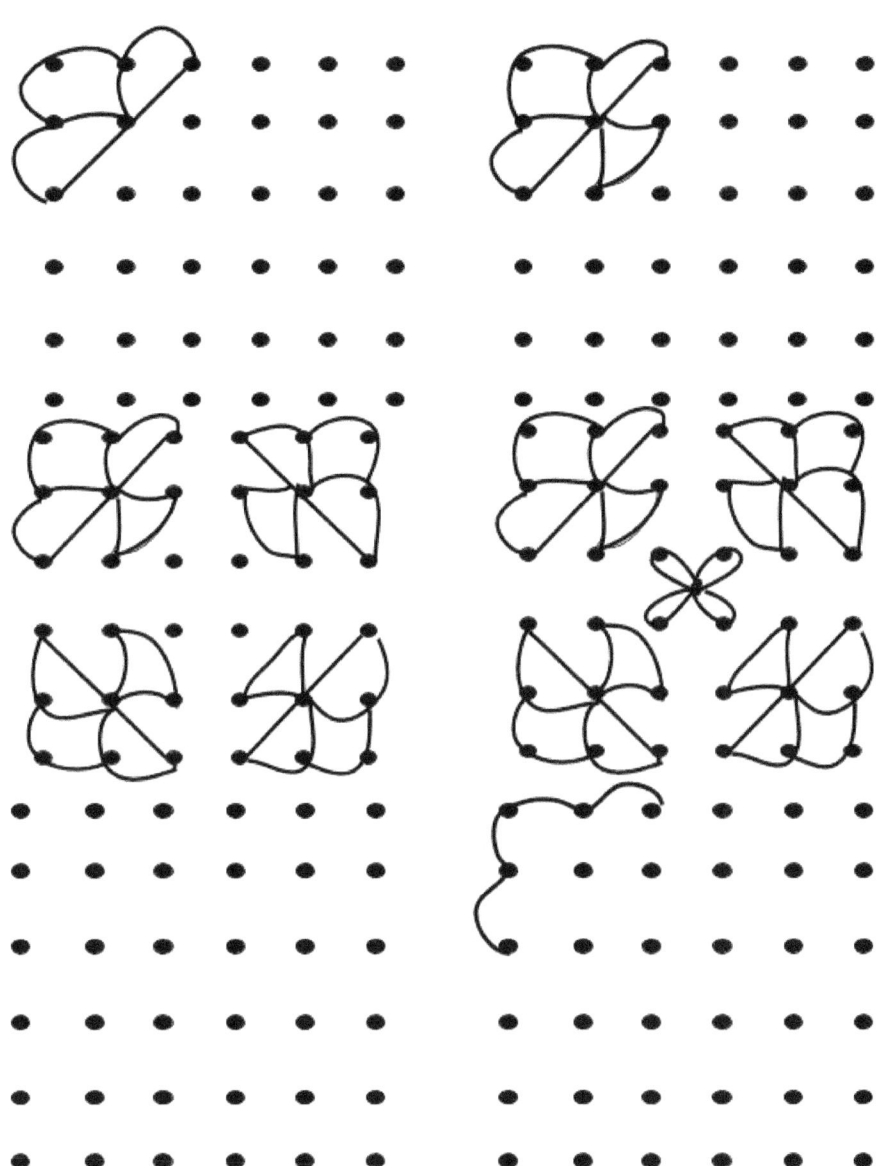

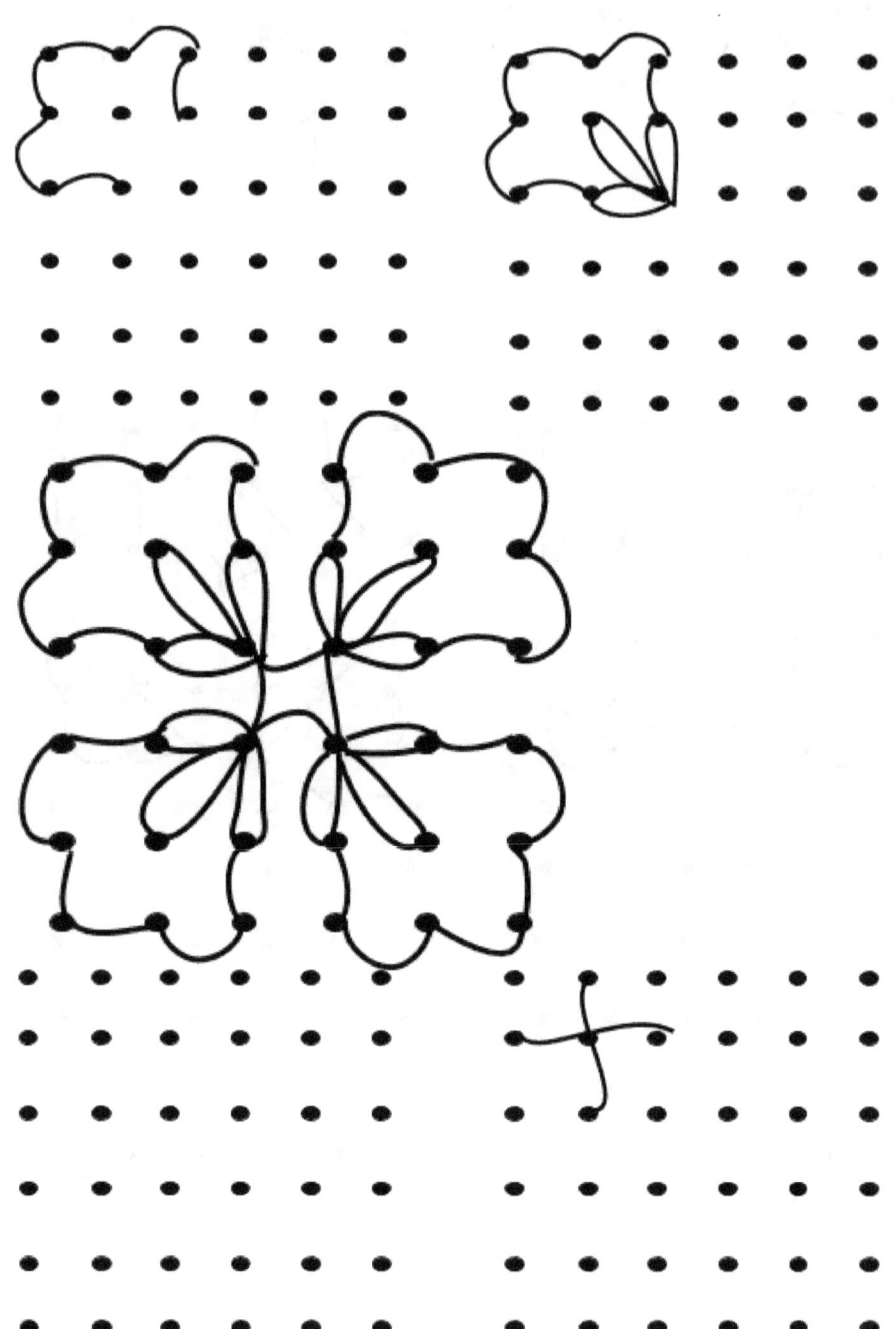

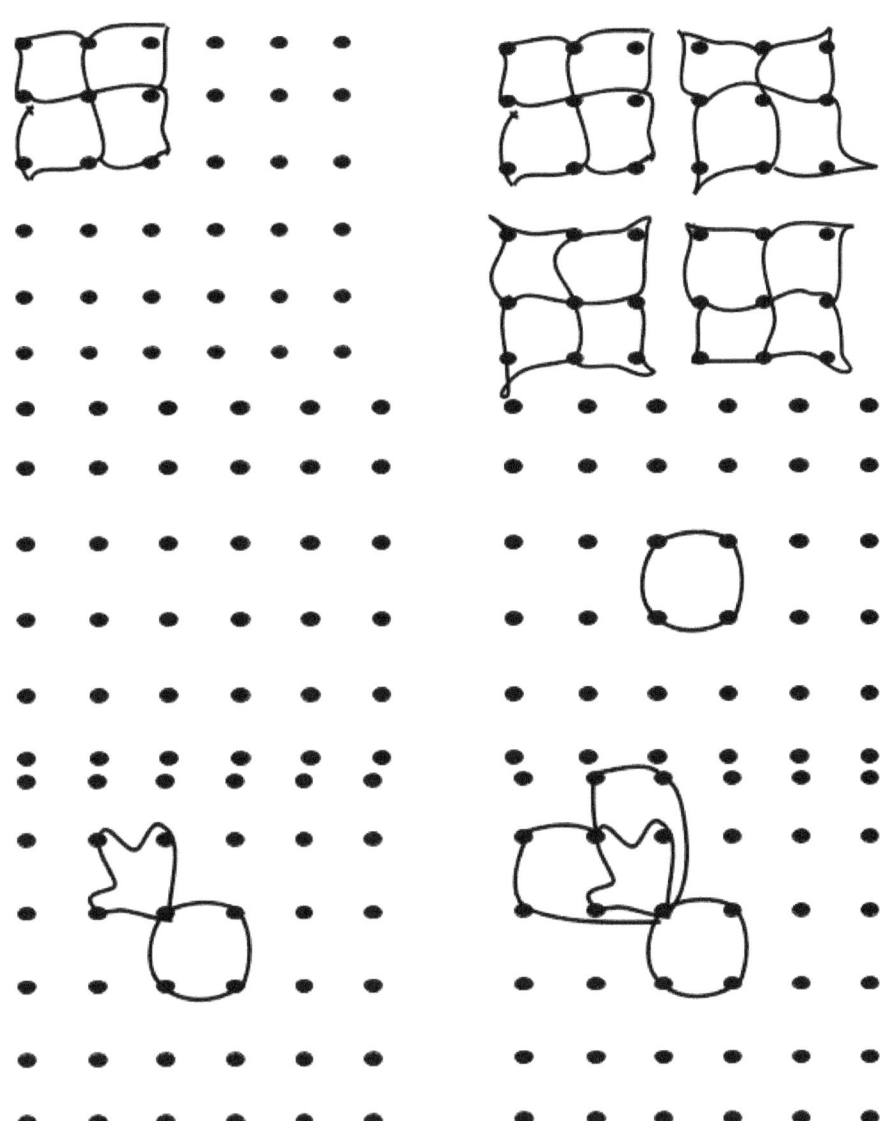

17

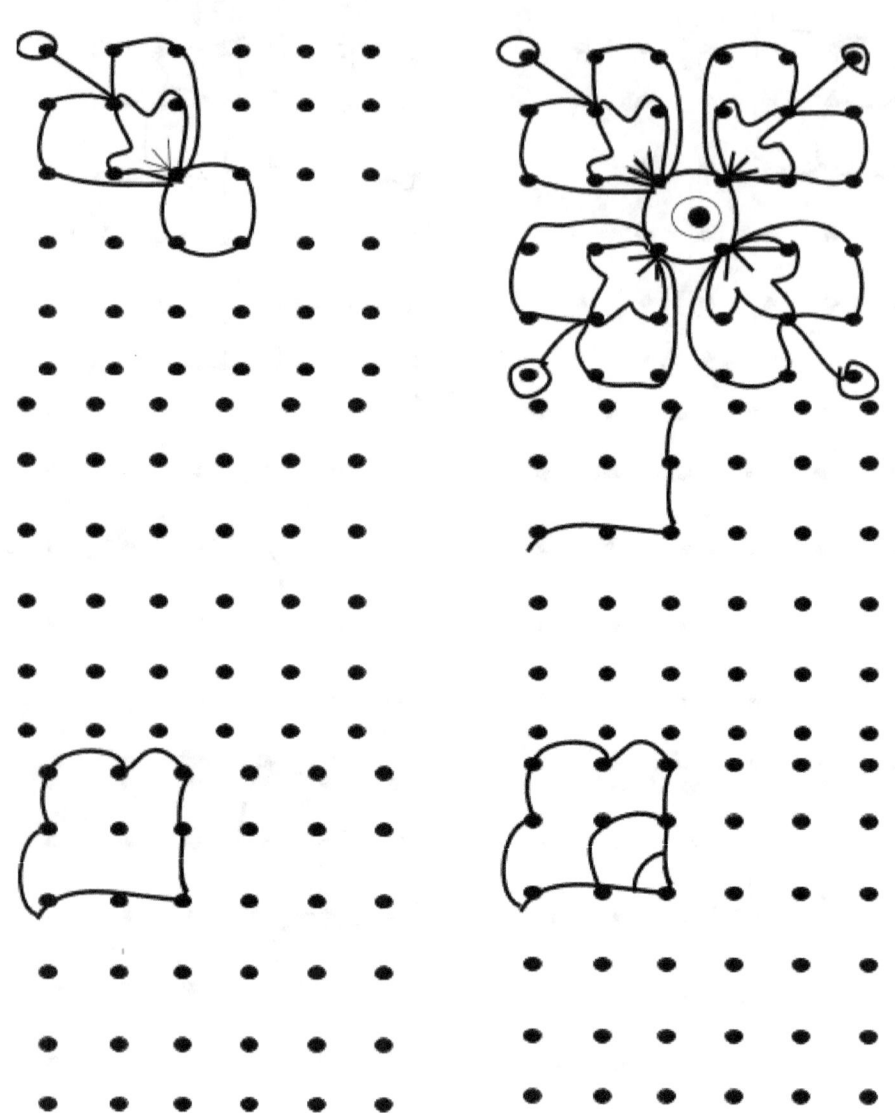

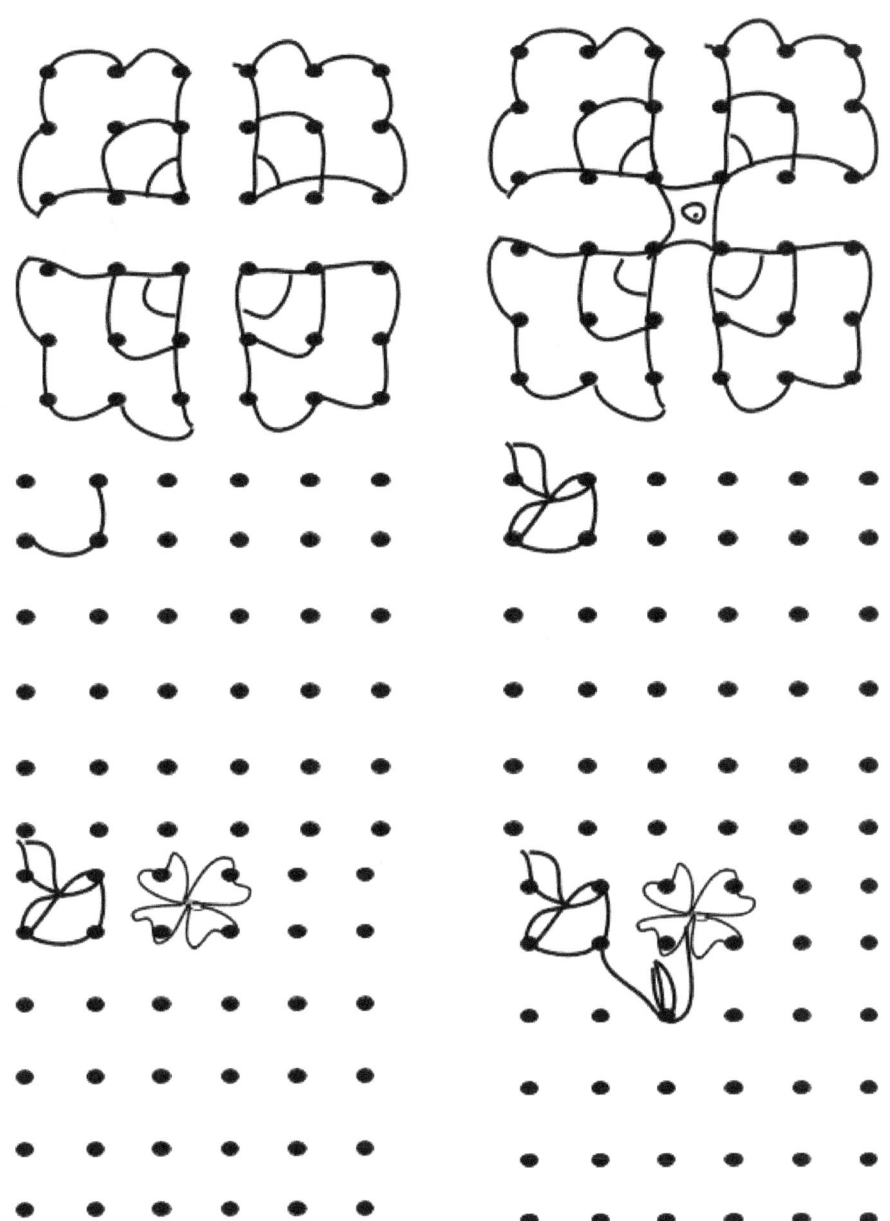

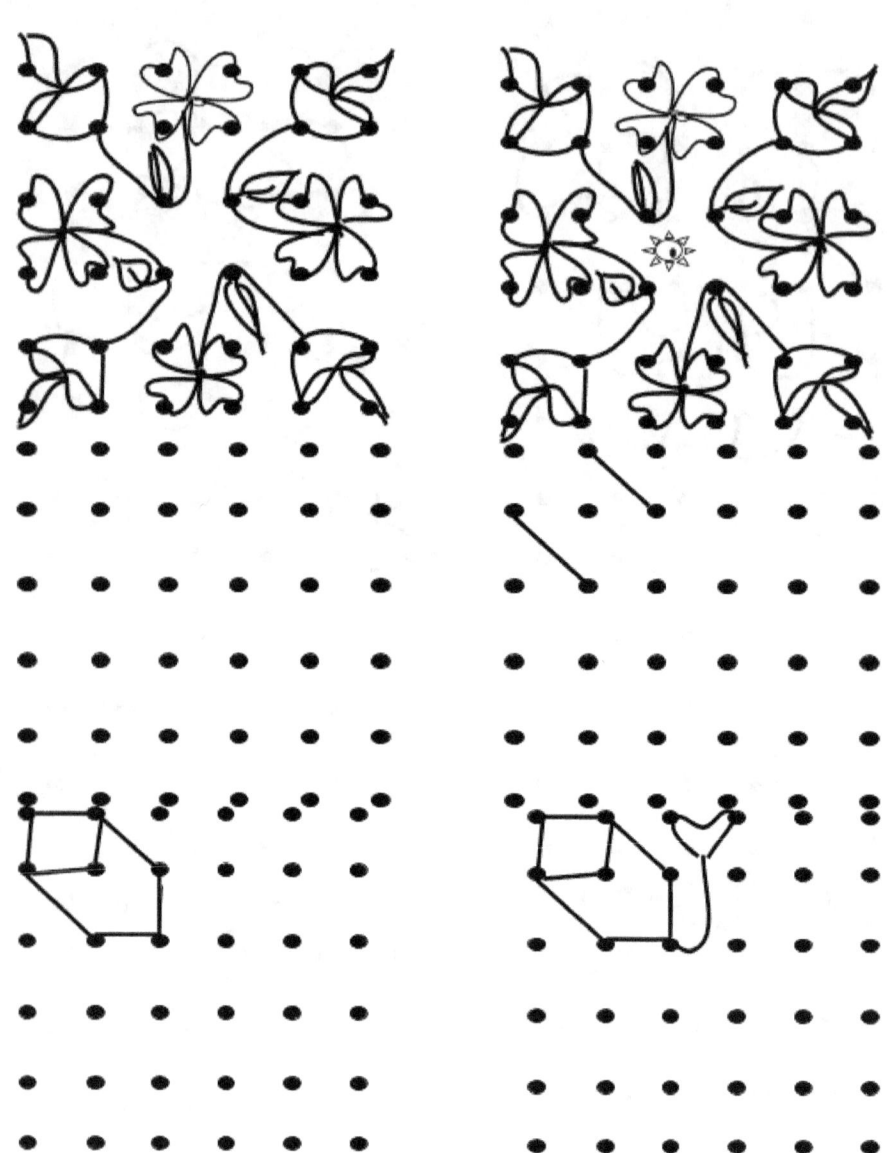

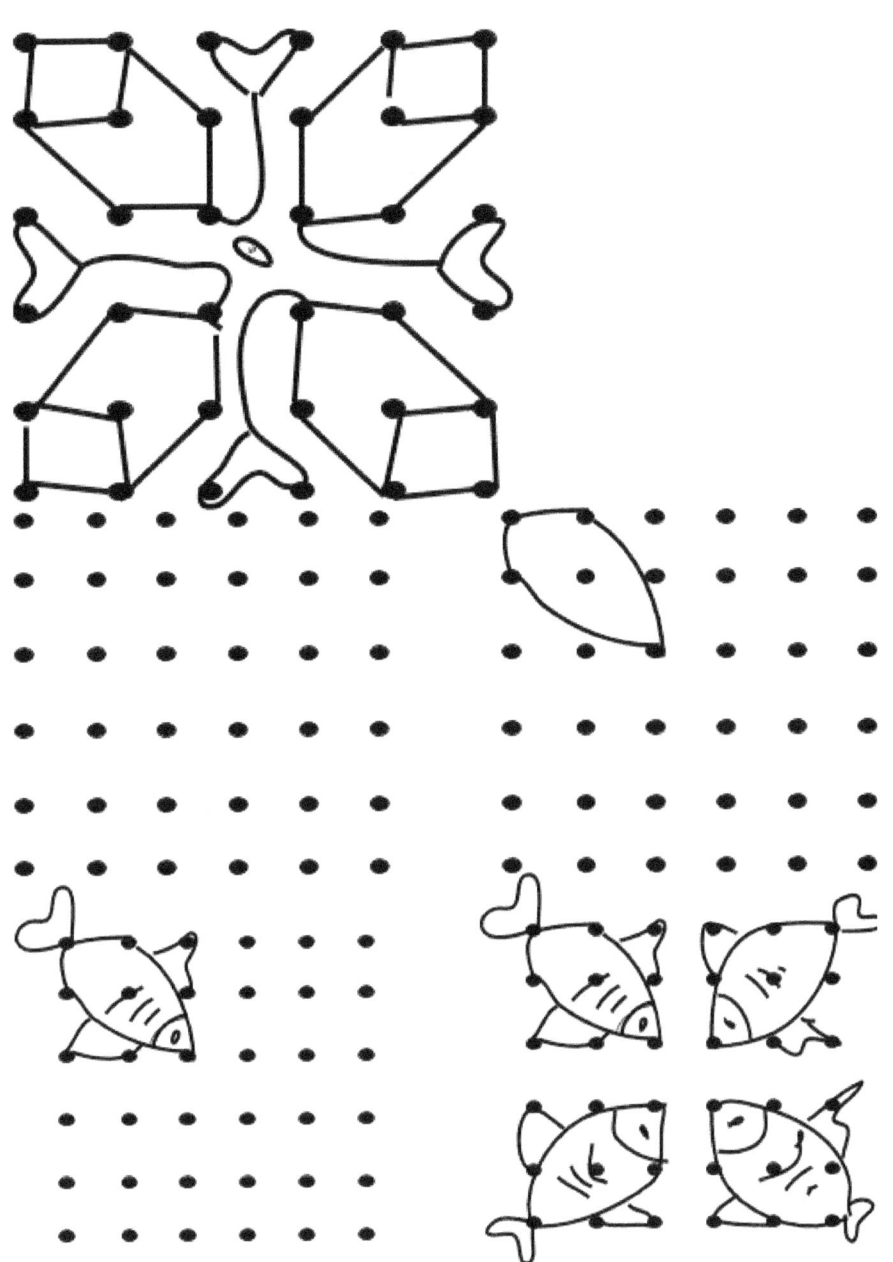

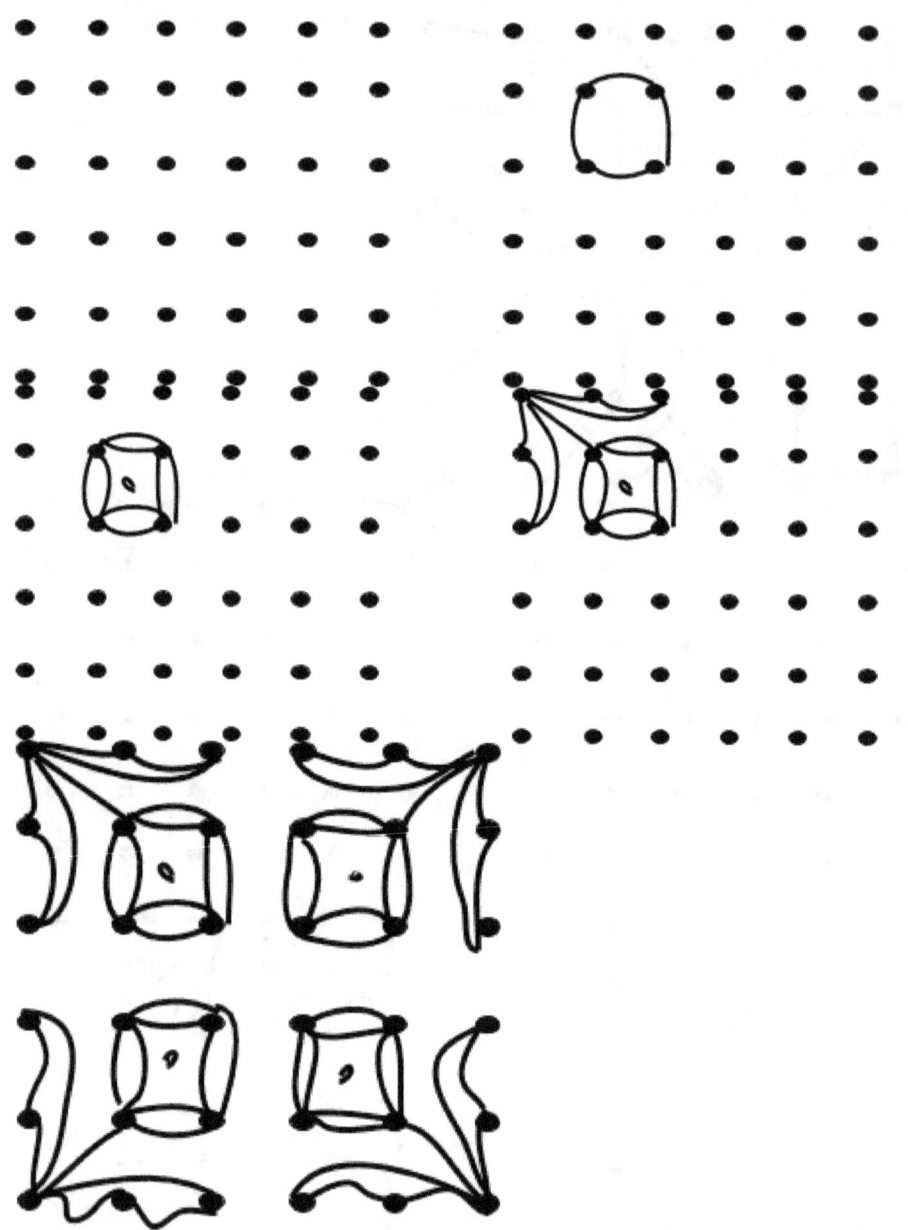

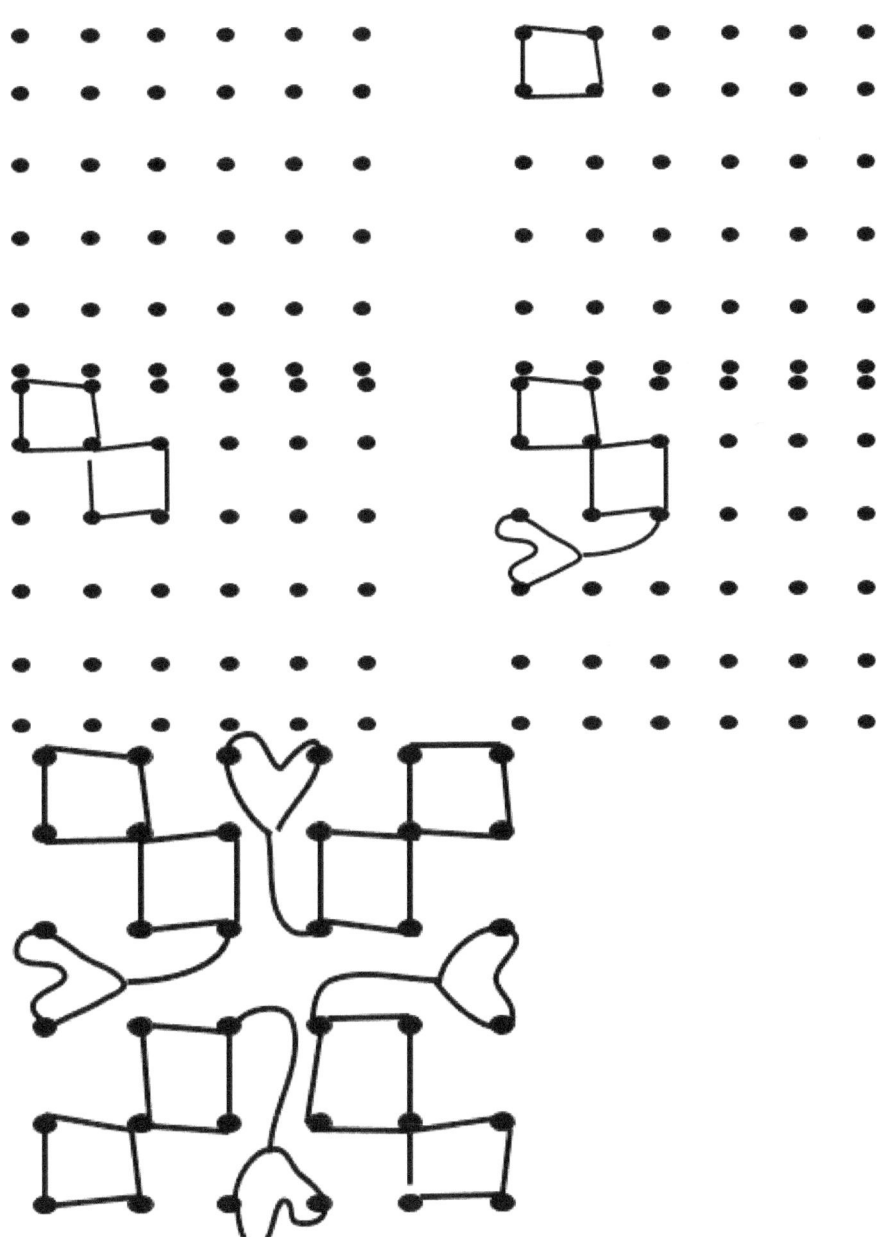

Worksheet.

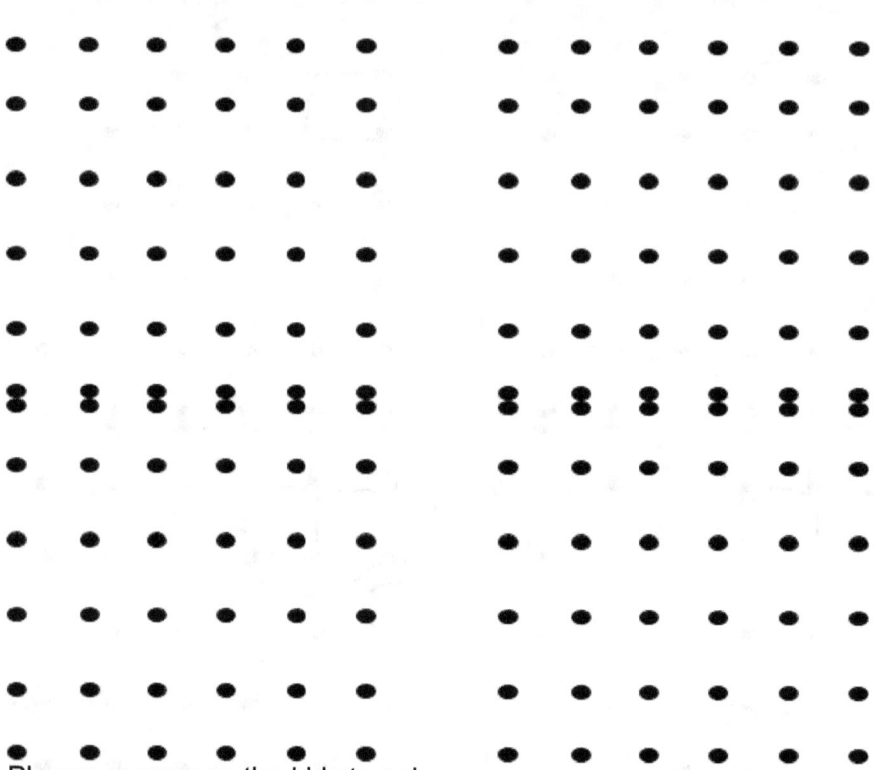

Please encourage the kids to color or draw the pictures.
Be happy.
Thank you.

www.ingramcontent.com/pod-product-compliance
Lightning Source LLC
Chambersburg PA
CBHW050329220526
45465CB00005B/2202